# JUSTICE LEAGUE UNLIMITED™
# DRAW-IT

written by **John Sazaklis**

 **studio** BOOKS

White Plains, New York • Montréal, Québec • Bath, United Kingdom

# Heroes Unite!

When planet Earth was invaded by evil aliens,
super heroes banded together to protect the
world. Superman saw great potential in the
group and he believed that they would be an
unbeatable team working for the ideals
of peace and justice. Thus, they combined
and formed the Justice League!

# How to Draw
# THE JUSTICE LEAGUE

This book has step-by-step instructions on how to draw twenty-three of your favorite DC super heroes and villains.

### Here are some tips:

For each character we show you a green line. This is called the Line of Action. It is an imaginary line that runs through your finished character. It helps you imagine the full shape and movement of your character. You can draw it if you want or just use it for a guide.

We also show Contour Lines on the character head. These are guidelines used to give the head dimension so it doesn't look so flat.

At the last step you can add details and go over your whole drawing with a darker pencil line or a pen.

### No matter what—have fun.
### It doesn't have to be perfect!

# How to Draw SUPERMAN

Born on the planet Krypton, Superman came to Earth as a baby. As he grew older, Superman developed many amazing abilities, thanks to the energy of the Earth's yellow Sun! He can fly, bend steel, and zoom faster than a speeding bullet. He also has heat vision and freeze breath! Superman uses all of his incredible powers to fight for truth and justice!

**1** Start with an action line. Then draw a small oval for the head and a large oval for the upper body.

**2** Map out the basic shapes of the arms using circles, ovals, and lines. Start to draw the details of the face and head.

**3** Draw an oval for the lower body. Map out the basic shapes of the legs using circles, ovals, and lines. Add details to the upper body.

**4**

Finish the body and add in the accessories.

**5**

Tighten up your sketch and include the final details. Don't forget the S-shield!

**The Man of Steel is ready to soar up, up, and away!**

# How to Draw BATMAN

Orphaned as a child, Batman vowed to fight crime and injustice in Gotham City. The Dark Knight has no superpowers, but his mind and body are highly trained. He is a scientist, martial arts expert, and inventor—with many high-tech gadgets and vehicles in his arsenal. Batman is also known as the World's Greatest Detective!

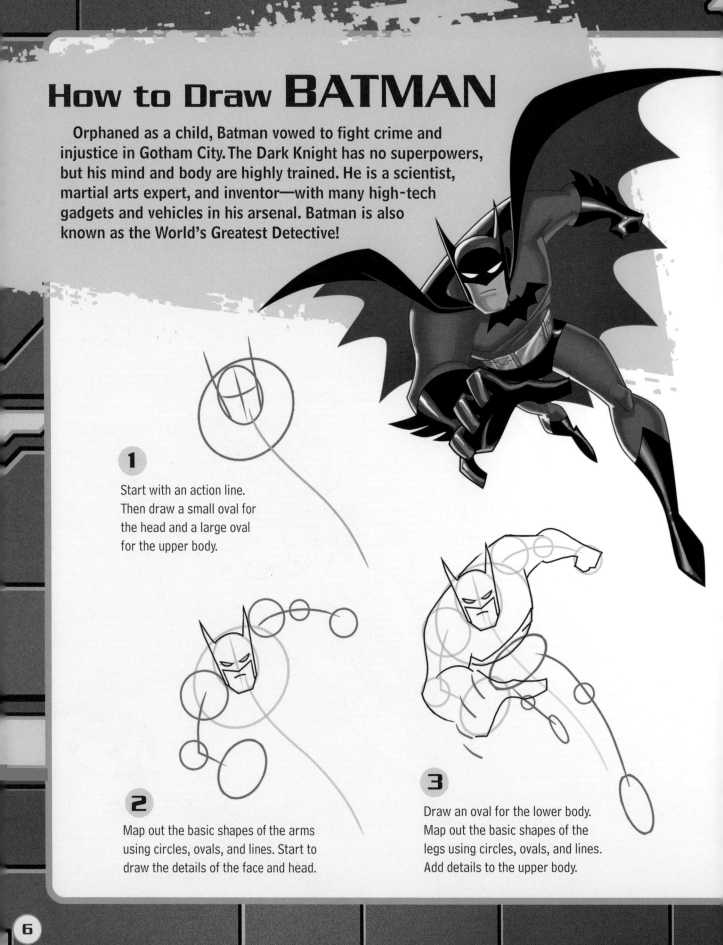

**1**

Start with an action line. Then draw a small oval for the head and a large oval for the upper body.

**2**

Map out the basic shapes of the arms using circles, ovals, and lines. Start to draw the details of the face and head.

**3**

Draw an oval for the lower body. Map out the basic shapes of the legs using circles, ovals, and lines. Add details to the upper body.

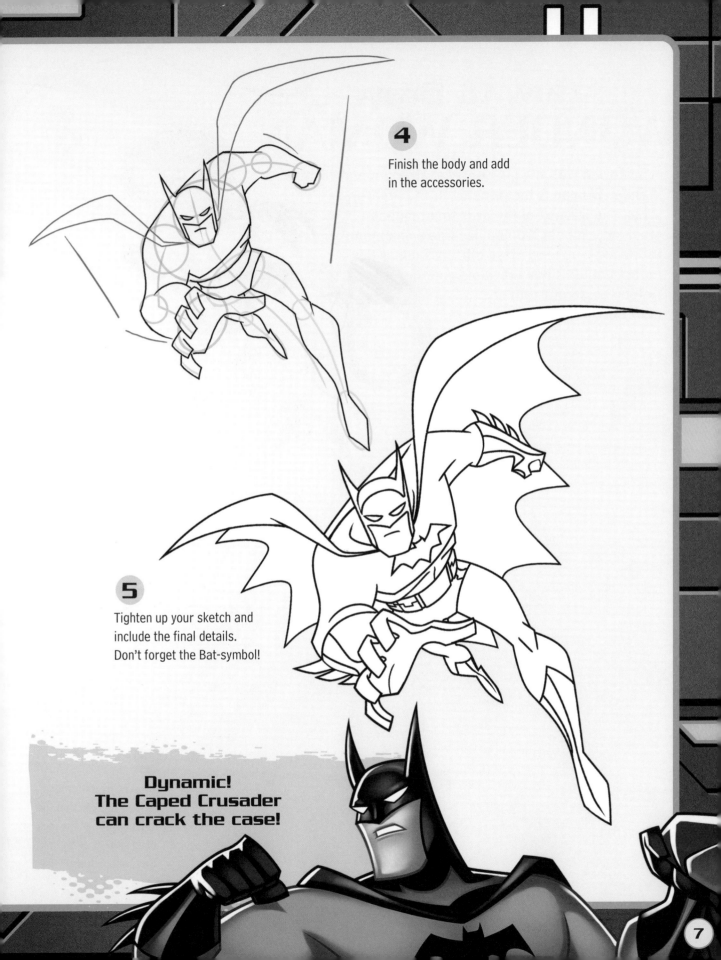

**4**

Finish the body and add in the accessories.

**5**

Tighten up your sketch and include the final details. Don't forget the Bat-symbol!

**Dynamic!
The Caped Crusader
can crack the case!**

# How to Draw
# WONDER WOMAN

Bestowed with the gifts of great strength and wisdom, Wonder Woman is the princess of the Amazons. When she learned of the evils that plagued mankind, Wonder Woman became a champion for peace. She uses these gifts, as well as her indestructible silver bracelets and Golden Lasso of Truth, in her quest for harmony.

**1**

Start with an action line. Then draw a small oval for the head and a large oval for the upper body.

**2**

Map out the basic shapes of the arms using circles, ovals, and lines. Start to draw the details of the face and head.

**3**

Draw an oval for the lower body. Map out the basic shapes of the legs using circles, ovals, and lines. Add details to the upper body.

**4**

Finish the body and add in the accessories.

**5**

Tighten up your sketch and include the final details. Don't forget the Golden Lasso of Truth!

**Wonderful! Wonder Woman is ready for action!**

# DESIGN YOUR OWN SUPER HERO!
### Use the stencils to complete his look!

# DESIGN YOUR OWN SUPER HERO!
## Is he super fast? Can he fly? Which stencils give him special powers?

# Justice for All

Known individually as some of the world's finest heroes, these courageous beings teamed up to become the Justice League. Brought together by Superman, each one has sworn to protect the universe from the forces of evil.

Complete this scene with the sticker stamps. Search for and find the correct sticker for each empty square.

# How to Draw
# GREEN LANTERN

This Galactic Guardian possesses strength and resolve, along with the Green Lantern power ring—an item that wields unlimited power! Anything Green Lantern imagines, the ring will create out of hard light energy. He can also use it to fly and build force fields, combining the forces of might and light!

**1** Start with an action line. Then draw a small oval for the head and a large oval for the upper body.

**2** Map out the basic shapes of the arms using circles, ovals, and lines. Start to draw the details of the face and head.

**3** Draw an oval for the lower body. Map out the basic shapes of the legs using circles, ovals, and lines. Add details to the upper body.

**4**

Finish the body and add in the accessories.

**5**

Tighten up your sketch and include the final details. Don't forget the Green Lantern force field!

**Great job! Green Lantern now lights the way!**

# How to Draw THE FLASH

The Flash was caught in a laboratory accident. It gave him the power to move incredibly fast, create whirlwinds by spinning in circles, and pass through solid objects by vibrating his molecules.

**1** Start with an action line. Then draw a small oval for the head and a large oval for the upper body.

**2** Map out the basic shapes of the arms using circles, ovals, and lines. Start to draw the details of the face and head.

**3** Draw an oval for the lower body. Map out the basic shapes of the legs using circles, ovals, and lines. Add details to the upper body.

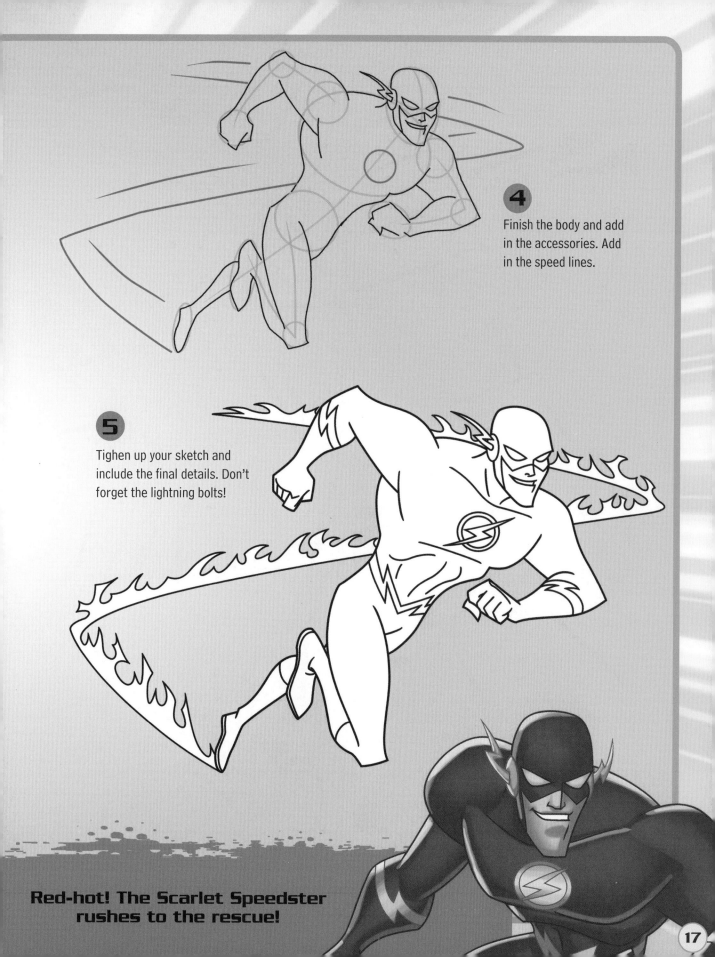

**4**

Finish the body and add in the accessories. Add in the speed lines.

**5**

Tighen up your sketch and include the final details. Don't forget the lightning bolts!

**Red-hot! The Scarlet Speedster rushes to the rescue!**

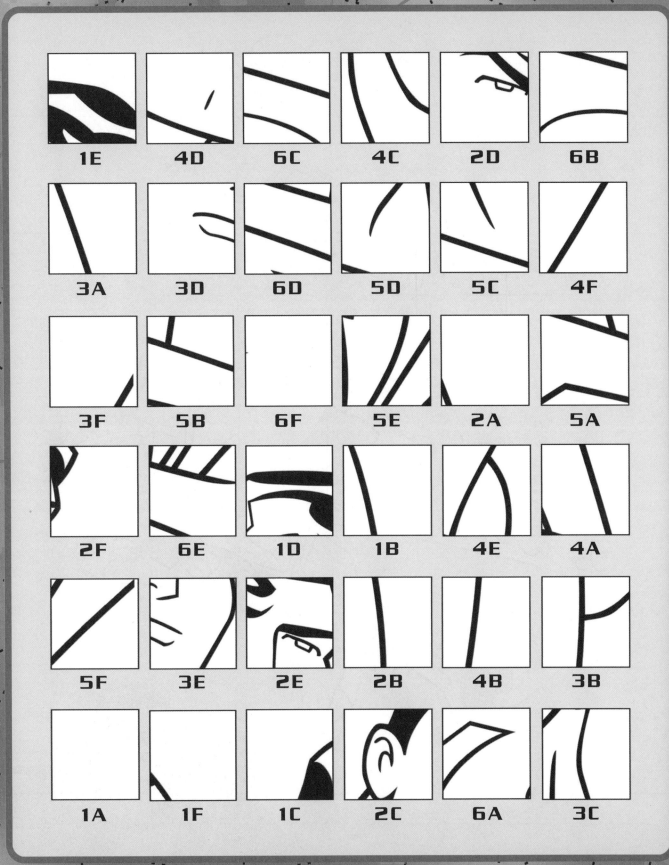

# Guess Who?

|   | A | B | C | D | E | F |
|---|---|---|---|---|---|---|
| 1 |   |   |   |   |   |   |
| 2 |   |   |   |   |   |   |
| 3 |   |   |   |   |   |   |
| 4 |   |   |   |   |   |   |
| 5 |   |   |   |   |   |   |
| 6 |   |   |   |   |   |   |

Who is known as the Man of Steel?
Complete this puzzle and you will find out.

Look at the number and letter under each square on the left page. Find the box on the empty grid above that matches the row number and the column letter.
Now copy the design you see in the square into the empty square.

This is a job for _____

# How to Draw MARTIAN MANHUNTER

Having left Mars long ago, Martian Manhunter made Earth his new home and fights alongside the Justice League. His superpowers are vast and impressive and include flight, invulnerability, and telepathy. Martian Manhunter is also a shape shifter, thus making his true identity a mystery!

**1**

Start with an action line. Then draw a small oval for the head and a large oval for the upper body.

**2**

Map out the basic shapes of the arms using circles, ovals, and lines. Start to draw the details of the face and head.

**3**

Draw an oval for the lower body. Map out the basic shapes of the legs using circles, ovals, and lines. Add details to the upper body.

**4**

Finish the body and add in the accessories.

**5**

Tighten up your sketch and include the final details. Don't forget the buccaneer boots!

**Martian Manhunter is out of this world!**

# How to Draw
# HAWKGIRL

A former lieutenant of the Thanagarian military, Hawkgirl is a skilled tactician and combatant, with higher levels of strength and endurance than humans. Her mighty wings grant her the ability to fly. She can also wield her Thanagarian mace, made of Nth Metal, with expert accuracy. It is her most prized possession!

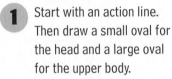

**1** Start with an action line. Then draw a small oval for the head and a large oval for the upper body.

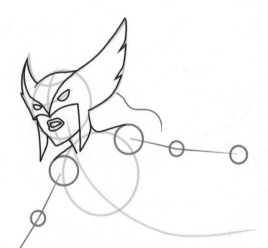

**2** Map out the basic shapes of the arms using circles, ovals, and lines. Start to draw the details of the face and head.

**3** Draw an oval for the lower body. Map out the basic shapes of the legs using circles, ovals, and lines. Add details to the upper body.

**4**

Finish the body and add in the accessories.

**5**

Tighten up your sketch and include the final details. Don't forget the feathers and mace!

**Excellent!
Hawkgirl is flying high!**

## ACCESSORIZE!
Does your super hero have a mask or helmet? Design it here and use the stencils to make it unique!

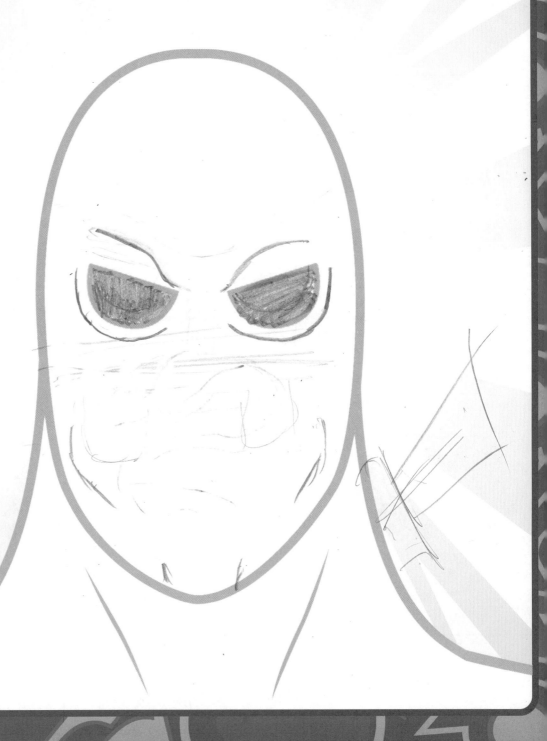

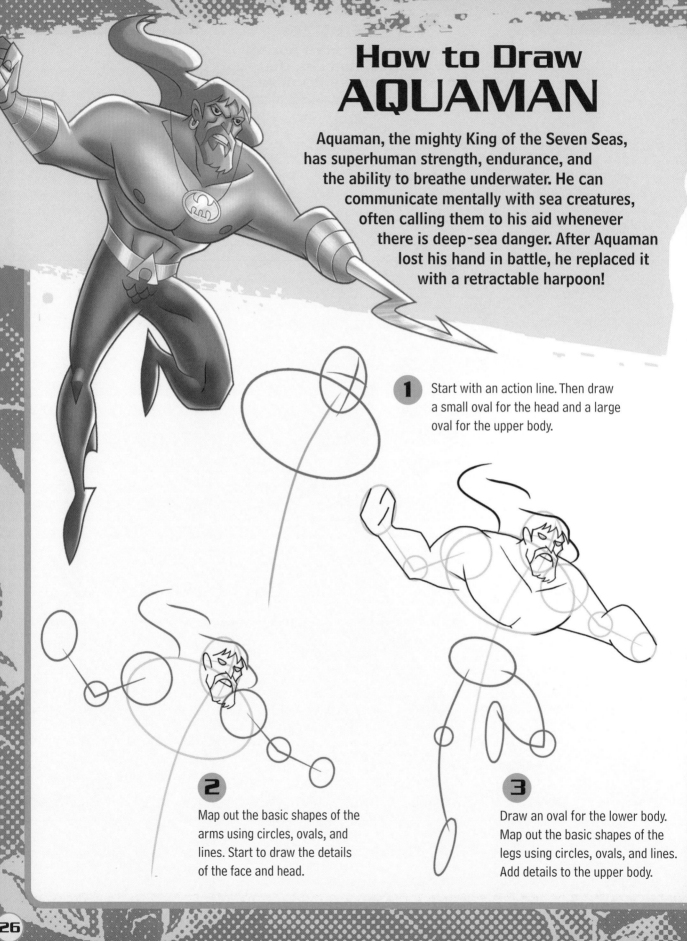

# How to Draw
# AQUAMAN

Aquaman, the mighty King of the Seven Seas, has superhuman strength, endurance, and the ability to breathe underwater. He can communicate mentally with sea creatures, often calling them to his aid whenever there is deep-sea danger. After Aquaman lost his hand in battle, he replaced it with a retractable harpoon!

**1** Start with an action line. Then draw a small oval for the head and a large oval for the upper body.

**2** Map out the basic shapes of the arms using circles, ovals, and lines. Start to draw the details of the face and head.

**3** Draw an oval for the lower body. Map out the basic shapes of the legs using circles, ovals, and lines. Add details to the upper body.

**4**

Finish the body and add in the accessories.

**5**

Tighten up your sketch and include the final details. Don't forget the beard and harpoon!

**Outstanding! Aquaman dives into action!**

# How to Draw
# GREEN ARROW

This suave, sophisticated businessman sold his billion-dollar company so that he could become a full-time vigilante. He became Green Arrow! Now the expert bowman fights for justice with his arsenal of trick arrows—his favorite one sports a boxing glove at the tip!

**1** Start with an action line. Then draw a small oval for the head and a large oval for the upper body.

**2** Map out the basic shapes of the arms using circles, ovals, and lines. Start to draw the details of the face and head.

**3** Draw an oval for the lower body. Map out the basic shapes of the legs using circles, ovals, and lines. Add details to the upper body.

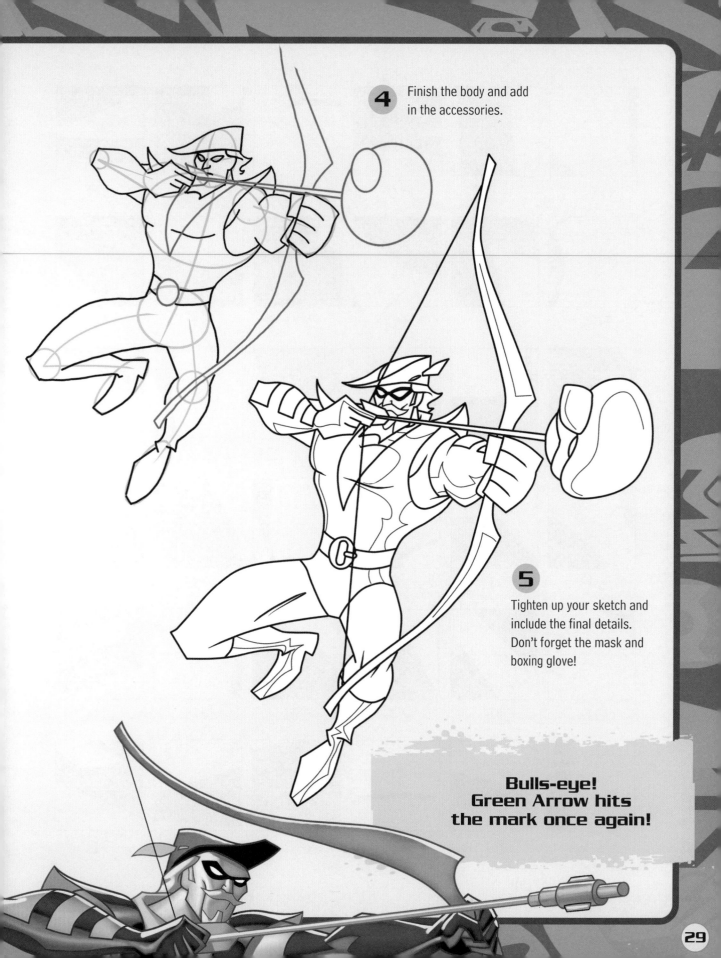

**4** Finish the body and add in the accessories.

**5** Tighten up your sketch and include the final details. Don't forget the mask and boxing glove!

**Bulls-eye! Green Arrow hits the mark once again!**

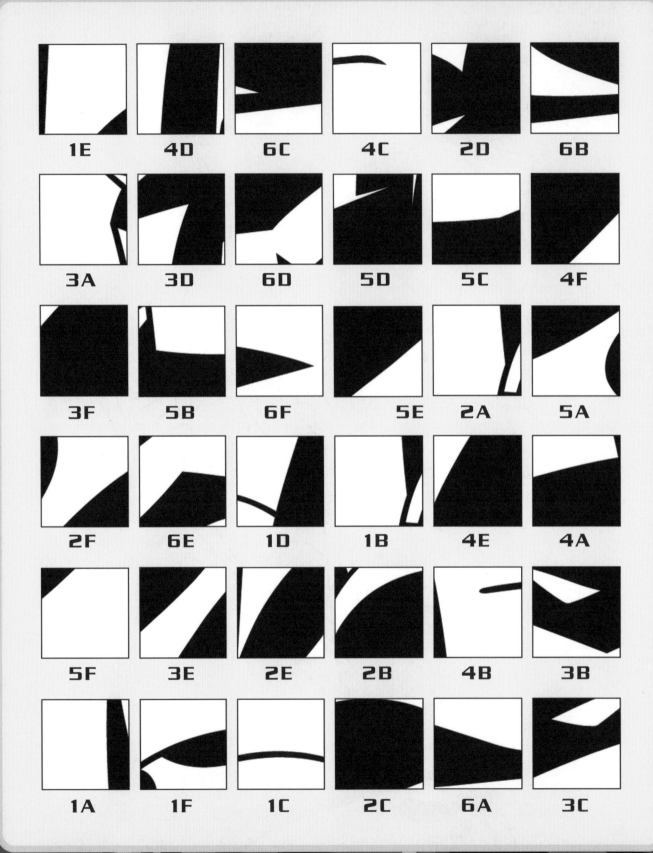

# Guess Who?

|   | A | B | C | D | E | F |
|---|---|---|---|---|---|---|
| 1 |   |   |   |   |   |   |
| 2 |   |   |   |   |   |   |
| 3 |   |   |   |   |   |   |
| 4 |   |   |   |   |   |   |
| 5 |   |   |   |   |   |   |
| 6 |   |   |   |   |   |   |

Which super hero is called the Dark Knight?
Complete this puzzle and you will find out.

Look at the number and letter under each square on the left page. Find the box on the empty grid above that matches the row number and the column letter. Now copy the design you see in the square into the empty square.

He's the World's Greatest Detective. He's _____

# How to Draw
# LEX LUTHOR

Extremely wealthy, Lex Luthor is one of the smartest businessmen in the world. He uses his scientific knowledge and vast resources to create dangerous devices, such as this high-tech power suit, to enhance his physical strength. His ultimate goal is to destroy the Justice League and gain control of the world!

**1**

Start with an action line. Then draw a small oval for the head and a large oval for the upper body.

**2**

Map out the basic shapes of the arms using circles, ovals, and lines. Start to draw the details of the face and head.

**3**

Draw an oval for the lower body. Map out the basic shapes of the legs using circles, ovals, and lines. Add details to the upper body.

**4**

Finish the body and add in the accessories.

**5**

Tighten up your sketch and include the final details. Don't forget the energy blasts!

**Look out! Lex Luthor plans to lay waste to Metropolis!**

# How to Draw
# THE JOKER

After falling into a vat of toxic chemicals, the Joker's appearance was severely altered. He now has chalk-white skin, green hair, and a permanent ruby smile! The Joker is a brilliant prank engineer with a twisted sense of humor. His weapons are deadly versions of party gags. Crossing his path is no laughing matter!

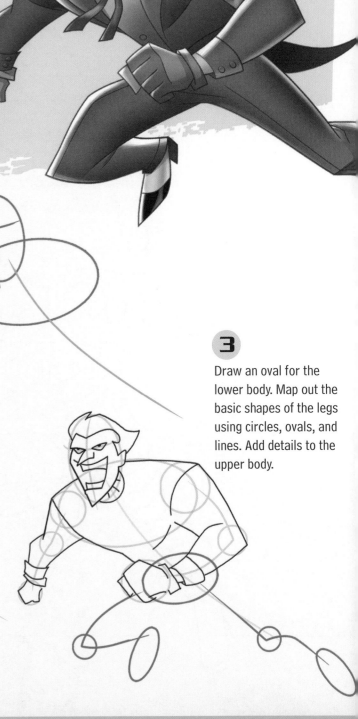

**1** Start with an action line. Then draw a small oval for the head and a large oval for the upper body.

**3** Draw an oval for the lower body. Map out the basic shapes of the legs using circles, ovals, and lines. Add details to the upper body.

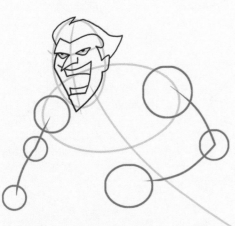

**2** Map out the basic shapes of the arms using circles, ovals, and lines. Start to draw the details of the face and head.

**4** Finish the body and add in the accessories.

**5**

Tighen up your sketch and include the final details. Don't forget the bowtie and acid-squirting flower!

**Jeepers! The Joker's criminal creep show will leave you in stitches—literally!**

# DESIGN YOUR OWN SUPER-VILLAIN
## Use the stencils to give this bad guy some extra punch!

# DESIGN YOUR OWN SUPER-VILLAIN
## Use the stencils to make him look even more menacing!

# Titans of Trouble

These vile villains stand against everything the Justice League believes in. Driven by pure evil, they will stop at nothing to bring forth chaos and destruction to the entire world. And they will do it with a smile!

Complete this scene with the sticker stamps. Search for and find the correct sticker for each empty square.

# How to Draw GORILLA GRODD

This proud and powerful primate is also a hyper-intelligent scientist with telepathic powers and enhanced senses. Armed with a diabolical weapon of his own creation, Gorilla Grodd is determined to enslave the entire human race by transforming them into apes—and then controlling them with his mind!

**1** Start with an action line. Then draw a small oval for the head and a large oval for the upper body.

**2** Map out the basic shapes of the arms using circles, ovals, and lines. Start to draw the details of the face and head.

**3** Draw an oval for the lower body. Map out the basic shapes of the legs using circles, ovals, and lines. Add details to the upper body.

**4**

Finish the body and add in the accessories.

**5**

Tighten up your sketch and include the final details. Don't forget the fur!

Don't make eye contact with Grodd, or else you will become his monkey minion!

# How to Draw
# DARKSEID

Darkseid is the monstrous ruler of Apokolips, and seeks to expand his dominion by conquering Earth. He can teleport across dimensions and his strength and speed rival that of Superman's! Most dangerous are his Omega Beams—red-hot lasers that shoot from his eyes, capable of incinerating anything in their path!

**1** Start with an action line. Then draw a small oval for the head and a large oval for the upper body.

**2** Map out the basic shapes of the arms using circles, ovals, and lines. Start to draw the details of the face and head.

**3** Draw an oval for the lower body. Map out the basic shapes of the legs using circles, ovals, and lines. Add details to the upper body.

**4**

Finish the body and add in the accessories.

**5**

Tighten up your sketch and include the final details. Don't forget the glowing red eyes!

**Danger!
Darkseid demands you
surrender your domain
to him...or else!**

Different letter styles express the different sounds you may hear. Here are some examples:

**A PUNCH**

**A LASER BLAST**

**MIND CONTROL**

**A BUILDING FALLING**

Different word balloon shapes express different things. Here are some examples:

**TALKING**

**THINKING**

**YELLING**

**CREEPY VOICE**

# Ready for Battle!

Whenever danger lurks, the Justice League is there! Using the stickers provided, create an epic battle between the forces of good and evil.

# How to Draw
# THE ATOM

The Atom is a physicist and professor who created a reducing ray using white dwarf star matter. He can shrink his body to varying degrees, travel through phone lines, and ride air currents. Even when tiny, the Atom retains all his full-size strength and packs a punch!

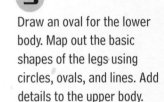

**1** Start with an action line. Then draw a small oval for the head and a large oval for the upper body.

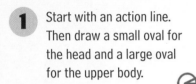

**2** Map out the basic shapes of the arms using circles, ovals, and lines. Start to draw the details of the face and head.

**3** Draw an oval for the lower body. Map out the basic shapes of the legs using circles, ovals, and lines. Add details to the upper body.

**4** Finish the body and add in the accessories.

**5** Tighten up your sketch and include the final details. Don't forget the mask!

**Titanic! Big things come in small packages!**